THE GENIUS KID'S GUIDE TO DOGS

BY MERRIAM GARCIA

North Star
KIDS

TABLE OF CONTENTS

HISTORY OF
DOMESTICATED DOGS

All dogs today are related to wolves. Some scientists think that between 15,000 and 40,000 years ago, dogs split from wolves. This split likely happened because of humans. There are a couple ideas as to how this started.

One idea is that people took wolf puppies for pets. Over time, these wolves became domesticated. Domesticated means to change from being wild to living with and helping people.

Another idea is that friendly wolves spent more time with humans than unfriendly wolves. The friendly wolves may have gotten food from humans. This would give them an advantage over unfriendly ones. Getting food easily could help them survive and have babies. Then, over time, the friendly wolves became domesticated. They wanted to be around people.

No matter which idea is right, some wolves started changing. They began to get the characteristics that people see in dogs today. They developed floppy ears and curly tails. They also started developing different coat colors. Scientists think these changes are connected to friendliness. In fact, scientists see friendliness as one genetic trait that's stronger in dogs than wolves. Dogs want to work with humans more than wolves do. They are more interested in what humans are doing. Also, dogs aren't as good at solving problems by themselves compared with wolves. Instead, dogs look to humans for help.

People started to breed dogs for specific purposes. Some people wanted a dog that could pull a heavy load for them or protect cattle. Others wanted a good hunting dog or a small companion. There are more than 340 dog breeds today. By late 2020, the American Kennel Club (AKC) acknowledged 195 of these breeds. The AKC is an organization that keeps a list of many purebred dogs. Purebred dogs come from one breed. Many other dogs aren't purebred. Instead, they are a combination of multiple breeds.

Dogs and wolves have the same ancestors.

Dogs in the herding group have been bred to help move animals. They do this by running, barking, and making eye contact with livestock in order to get the animals from one spot to another. For example, corgis are small, but they nip at cattle's feet to get them moving. Today, most herding dogs don't live on farms. However, they still have an instinct to herd whatever is around them. Sometimes, they will run circles around people to try and round them up.

German shepherd dog

Border collie

AUSTRALIAN CATTLE DOG AKC DATE: 1980

APPEARANCE

An Australian cattle dog's (ACD) fur is beautiful, low maintenance, and weatherproof. This breed's hardy fur can be blue or red.

- **Height:** 17 to 20 inches (43 to 51 cm)
- **Weight:** 35 to 50 pounds (16 to 23 kg)

DID YOU KNOW?

Every ACD sheds its undercoat once or twice a year.

BEHAVIOR

The ACD was bred for long hours of hard labor and hates to sit still. Without a challenging job, it can become bored and destructive. The ACD is highly intelligent and eager to learn. As a natural watchdog, it is wary of strangers. But it is loyal, loving, and faithful to its family.

BREED HISTORY

In the 1800s, Australian settlers developed a strong herding dog. Two decades later, this dog breed was bred with Dalmatians and Australian kelpies to make the ACD.

SPECIAL CONSIDERATIONS

This breed needs a firm leader, love, attention, and exercise.

AUSTRALIAN SHEPHERD AKC DATE: 1991

APPEARANCE

An Australian shepherd's fur is straight to wavy. Its coat can be blue merle, black, red merle, or red. They may have white or tan markings, too.

- **Height:** 18 to 23 inches (46 to 58 cm)
- **Weight:** 40 to 65 pounds (18 to 30 kg)

DID YOU KNOW?

If an Aussie has a merle coat, it might become darker with age.

BEHAVIOR

The Australian shepherd lives to work. It was bred for herding and guarding. If well socialized, an Aussie will get along with other animals.

BREED HISTORY

Australian shepherds began as expert farm and ranch dogs in the United States. Today, they have additional jobs. Aussies work as service dogs and therapy dogs. They help sniff out drugs. They also perform search and rescue missions.

SPECIAL CONSIDERATIONS

This breed likes to chew, so be sure to have safe toys for them to play with.

BORDER COLLIE AKC DATE: 1995

APPEARANCE

The Border collie has a thick double coat. It can be black and white. Some coats are black, brown, and white. Other coat colors and patterns are slate gray, tan, brindle, fawn, blue, blue merle, red, red merle, and lilac.

- **Height:** 18 to 22 inches (46 to 56 cm)
- **Weight:** 30 to 55 pounds (14 to 25 kg)

DID YOU KNOW?

This breed's eyes can be brown or blue. Some dogs have one blue eye and one brown eye.

BEHAVIOR

Border collies are incredibly smart and usually friendly. They may be wary of strangers, but they love their families.

SPECIAL CONSIDERATIONS

This breed is active and needs exercise.

BREED HISTORY

In Scotland, dogs originally called Scotch sheep dogs were popular with shepherds. Some of these dogs lived along the border of Scotland and England. Eventually they became known as Border collies.

CATAHOULA LEOPARD DOG AKC DATE: AWAITING

APPEARANCE

The Catahoula leopard dog's coat is short. Some Catahoula leopard dog coats have the distinctive merle pattern. Others are solid red, yellow, black, or chocolate. They may also have brindle coats.

- **Height:** 22 to 24 inches (56 to 61 cm)
- **Weight:** 50 to 95 pounds (23 to 43 kg)

BEHAVIOR

Catahoula leopard dogs are very smart. They like to investigate new situations and have a lot of energy. Catahoula leopard dogs are very protective. It might take them a while to accept strangers.

DID YOU KNOW?

The Catahoula leopard dog is known for its light blue eyes. But this breed may also have amber, green, or brown eyes. Sometimes, each eye is a different color.

SPECIAL CONSIDERATIONS

Catahoulas need to know that their owners are in charge. Otherwise, they can be destructive or aggressive and get into trouble.

BREED HISTORY

No one knows for sure what the history is of the Catahoula leopard dog. Some believe this breed descended from large mastiffs, bloodhounds, and greyhounds.

COLLIE AKC DATE: 1885

APPEARANCE

Collies come in two types. There are smooth-coated collies and rough-coated collies. Collies can be sable and white or tricolor, which is black, tan, and white. They can also have a white body with a bit of color on the head. Or they can be blue merle. This is a mostly blue-gray coat with black and white markings.

- **Height:** 22 to 26 inches (56 to 66 cm)
- **Weight:** 50 to 75 pounds (23 to 34 kg)

DID YOU KNOW?

Collies are loyal and nurturing. They bond with all members of the family. They are especially good with children.

BEHAVIOR

Collies are smart dogs. When well trained, these dogs can understand and obey many commands.

SPECIAL CONSIDERATIONS
This breed needs exercise and frequent grooming.

BREED HISTORY
In the 1860s, Queen Victoria visited Scotland. She fell in love with the intelligent collie. She returned to London, England, with a few collies. Soon, the breed's popularity spread across England.

GERMAN SHEPHERD DOG AKC DATE: 1908

APPEARANCE

The German shepherd dog has straight, medium-length hair. It comes in various colors. The most common coat colors are black and tan or black and red.

- **Height:** 22 to 26 inches (56 to 66 cm)
- **Weight:** 50 to 90 pounds (23 to 41 kg)

DID YOU KNOW?

German shepherds love children and happily guard their homes and humans.

BEHAVIOR

German shepherds are smart and take well to training. Their intelligence makes them useful on police teams as well as search and rescue missions.

German shepherds have a desire to work and are faithful companions. They make excellent service animals for people who are blind or people with disabilities. German shepherds are loyal, dependable dogs.

BREED HISTORY

The German shepherd is a fairly young breed. It originated in the late 1800s. The German shepherd's ancestors were herding and farm dogs. Like its ancestors, the German shepherd still herds sheep.

SPECIAL CONSIDERATIONS

This breed needs exercise and attention.

OLD ENGLISH SHEEPDOG AKC DATE: 1888

APPEARANCE

The Old English sheepdog's coat can be many different colors, such as blue and white, gray and white, and blue merle and white. The Old English sheepdog's eyes can be blue or brown. Some have one eye of each color.

- **Height:** Around 21 inches and up (53 cm)
- **Weight:** 60 to 100 pounds (27 to 45 kg)

DID YOU KNOW?

It is very important to groom Old English sheepdogs every day or two. A matted coat may cause skin problems.

BEHAVIOR

Old English sheepdogs are happy dogs with an even nature. They love to play and want to be part of the family. Old English sheepdogs are energetic and love attention.

BREED HISTORY

The Old English sheepdog's beginnings are lost to history. However, the Old English sheepdog was developed in western England. The breed can be traced back to the early 1800s.

SHETLAND SHEEPDOG AKC DATE: 1911

APPEARANCE

Shetland sheepdogs, or shelties, can have many colors in their coats. Some colors and patterns are black, sable, and blue merle. They are often marked with white or tan.

- **Height:** 13 to 16 inches (33 to 40 cm)
- **Weight:** 15 to 25 pounds (7 to 11 kg)

DID YOU KNOW?

These playful dogs are easy to train and love to please their owners. They can be taught to put away their own toys on command.

BEHAVIOR

Shetland sheepdogs are highly intelligent. They are also loyal. They want to be close to their owners and do not like to be left alone.

SPECIAL CONSIDERATIONS

This breed needs to be exercised and played with.

BREED HISTORY

The Border collie was bred with a small island dog called the yakki. Later, it also bred with the English toy spaniel and the Pomeranian. In time, these mixed-breed dogs developed into a new breed called the Shetland sheepdog.

CARDIGAN WELSH CORGI AKC DATE: 1935

APPEARANCE

Cardigan Welsh corgis have a long tail. Their ears are big with round tips. Their front legs are slightly bowed, so their toes point outward. Their coats can be red, sable, brindle, black, and blue merle.

- **Height:** 10.5 to 12.5 inches (27 to 32 cm)
- **Weight:** 25 to 38 pounds (11 to 17 kg)

DID YOU KNOW?

Corgi coats shed. This is most noticeable in spring and fall.

BREED HISTORY

Welsh corgis come from Wales in the United Kingdom. The Cardigan Welsh corgi is from Cardiganshire. Cardigan corgi ancestors came to Wales from central Europe.

BEHAVIOR

Both corgi breeds are loving, protective, alert, smart, and easily trained. They make wonderful family companions and want to be involved in family activities.

Corgis were bred to work on farms. Many early farmers had flocks of geese or chickens that wandered freely. Corgis were trained to herd these birds. They also rid farms of rats and other unwanted creatures.

PEMBROKE WELSH CORGI AKC DATE: 1934

APPEARANCE

Pembroke Welsh corgis have a wide variety of coat colors. These include red, dark brown, black and tan, yellow brown, black and white, and blue. Pembroke corgis have shorter tails and smaller, more pointed ears than Cardigans. Pembrokes also have straight front legs.

- **Height:** 10 to 12 inches (25 to 30 cm)
- **Weight:** 28 to 30 pounds (13 to 14 kg)

DID YOU KNOW?

Though the Cardigan is the older breed, there are more Pembroke corgis.

BREED HISTORY

The Pembroke Welsh corgi is from Pembrokeshire. Pembroke corgi roots go back to the year 1107. At that time, Flemish weavers brought Schipperke and Pomeranian dogs to Wales. Their descendants developed into the Pembroke corgi.

SPECIAL CONSIDERATIONS

It is easy for corgis to gain weight, so exercise is important. These dogs also love to play.

ADDITIONAL BREEDS IN THE GROUP

BEARDED COLLIE

- **What It's Known For:** Moving livestock
- **Where It Comes From:** Scotland
- **Special Considerations:** This breed is willful and independent.

BEAUCERON

- **What It's Known For:** Herding
- **Where It Comes From:** France
- **Special Considerations:** This breed sheds a lot.

BELGIAN SHEEPDOG

- **What It's Known For:** Herding
- **Where It Comes From:** Belgium
- **Special Considerations:** This breed needs lots of attention.

Bearded collie

Bergamasco sheepdog

BERGAMASCO SHEEPDOG

- **What It's Known For:** Guarding and herding sheep
- **Where It Comes From:** Italy
- **Special Considerations:** This breed is intelligent and needs attention.

BERGER PICARD

- **What It's Known For:** Herding
- **Where It Comes From:** France
- **Special Considerations:** This breed can be stubborn.

Berger Picard

ADDITIONAL BREEDS IN THE GROUP

CANAAN DOG

- **What It's Known For:** Herding and guarding
- **Where It Comes From:** Middle East
- **Special Considerations:** These dogs enjoy digging and can also be territorial.

ENTLEBUCHER MOUNTAIN DOG

- **What It's Known For:** Moving cattle
- **Where It Comes From:** Switzerland
- **Special Considerations:** This breed is independent and energetic.

FINNISH LAPPHUND

- **What It's Known For:** Herding reindeer
- **Where It Comes From:** Finland
- **Special Considerations:** These dogs have an instinct to bark and are strong-willed.

Finnish Lapphund

ICELANDIC SHEEPDOG

- **What It's Known For:** Herding
- **Where It Comes From:** Iceland
- **Special Considerations:** This breed will bark and is curious.

POLISH LOWLAND SHEEPDOG

- **What It's Known For:** Herding and guarding
- **Where It Comes From:** Poland
- **Special Considerations:** This breed can be stubborn.

SPANISH WATER DOG

- **What It's Known For:** Herding and retrieving
- **Where It Comes From:** Unknown
- **Special Considerations:** These dogs have lots of energy and need exercise.

Polish lowland sheepdog

HOUND DOGS

Dogs in the hound group were bred to help hunters catch prey. These dogs either have a good sense of smell or are fast. This group of dogs is diverse. Some hounds are lanky and tall while others have short legs. Dogs in this group can have long or short hair and come in many colors. And some hounds can make a distinct baying sound. Today, some hounds are still used for hunting. But they also make wonderful companions for families.

Greyhound

Beagle

BASSET HOUND AKC DATE: 1885

APPEARANCE

A basset hound's coat is useful when hunting. It protects the basset from the scrapes of branches in the field. Underneath their coats, basset hounds have loose skin. The loose skin around a basset's nose helps the dog gather scents.

- **Height:** up to 15 inches (38 cm)
- **Weight:** 40 to 65 pounds (18 to 29 kg)

DID YOU KNOW?

Bassets have very long ears. When bassets are trailing prey, their ears often drag on the ground and stir up scents.

BEHAVIOR

Basset hounds are friendly dogs that love children. They can also be very stubborn. This makes it hard for them to be trained. So basset owners must be patient during training sessions.

SPECIAL CONSIDERATIONS

A basset hound's ears can become infected easily. It is important to keep a basset's ears clean.

BREED HISTORY

The basset hound has been around since the 1500s. It was first bred in France to trail small animals such as rabbits.

BEAGLE AKC DATE: 1885

APPEARANCE

Beagles have short, smooth double coats. Beagles can be any combination of colors, such as white, black, tan, lemon, blue-gray, or red-brown. Beagles are one of two sizes.

- **Height:** Under 13 inches (33 cm) or between 13 and 15 inches (33 and 38 cm)
- **Weight:** Smaller beagles are usually under 20 pounds (9 kg). Larger beagles are about 20 to 30 pounds (9 to 14 kg)

DID YOU KNOW?

Beagles have bold attitudes and like to be part of a pack. They are happiest when they are with other pets or their families.

BEHAVIOR

Beagles will sometimes run off to follow a scent. They are also independent. It can be difficult to keep them focused on training.

SPECIAL CONSIDERATIONS

These dogs prefer to be with their families for most of the day. If they are unsupervised for long periods of time, they can get into trouble. This includes a lot of barking and howling.

BREED HISTORY

Early beagles assisted English hunters with finding rabbits. Originally, there were rough-coated and smooth-coated beagles. The size of the dogs varied greatly. After the US Civil War (1861–1865), US breeders began to import beagles from England. They began to create a standard beagle type.

BLOODHOUND AKC DATE: 1885

APPEARANCE

A bloodhound has thin, loose skin. It hangs in folds around the dog's head, neck, and mouth. A bloodhound's coat can be black and tan; grayish, reddish brown and tan; or solid red in color.

- **Height:** 23 to 27 inches (58 to 69 cm)
- **Weight:** 80 to 110 pounds (36 to 50 kg)

DID YOU KNOW?

Bloodhounds love to track scents. They enjoy it so much that sometimes they don't pay any attention to their owners. This quality can sometimes make bloodhounds difficult to train.

BEHAVIOR

Bloodhounds are fairly large dogs, but they are good-natured animals. Bloodhounds are shy, gentle, and friendly. They are also a little messy, because they often drool.

SPECIAL CONSIDERATIONS

Because they are so big, bloodhounds need plenty of space to roam.

BREED HISTORY

The bloodhound breed began hundreds of years ago. Monks at St. Hubert's monastery in Belgium bred these hounds as early as the 1000s. There, they were known as St. Huberts.

BLUETICK COONHOUND AKC DATE: 2009

APPEARANCE

The bluetick coat is short, glossy, and very colorful. Every bluetick has thick, dark-blue ticked fur on its body. This freckled blue-and-white pattern gave the bluetick its name.

- **Height:** 21 to 27 inches (53 to 69 cm)
- **Weight:** 45 to 80 pounds (20 to 36 kg)

DID YOU KNOW?

Blueticks give off a strong, musty scent. This is common for certain hound breeds. Even if you bathe a bluetick, its scent won't disappear completely. Yet many people grow to love this "houndy" smell.

BEHAVIOR

The bluetick coonhound is a big bundle of energy. It is also very intelligent. Although the bluetick can be stubborn, it is also eager to please. Praise and food rewards can be used to train this breed.

BREED HISTORY

Bluetick coonhounds were specially bred to hunt. They originated from a mix of breeds, including the English foxhound.

SPECIAL CONSIDERATIONS

This breed is not recommended for apartments. The bluetick coonhound was bred to be noisy. Each one has a special bawl used to alert hunters of a trail.

DACHSHUND AKC DATE: 1885

APPEARANCE

There are three types of coats for the dachshund. They are smooth, longhair, and wirehair. Smooth dachshunds have glossy hair, and their coats are short all over. The outercoat of the longhaired dachshund is glossy and wavy. The wirehaired variety has a soft undercoat. The outercoat is short, hard, and wiry. This breed comes in two sizes. These are standard and miniature.

Standard dachshunds
- **Height:** 8 to 9 inches (20 to 23 cm)
- **Weight:** 16 to 32 pounds (7 to 15 kg)

Miniature dachshunds
- **Height:** 5 to 6 inches (13 to 15 cm)
- **Weight:** 11 pounds (5 kg) or less

DID YOU KNOW?

Dachshunds are short. They were bred to have long, muscular bodies.

BEHAVIOR

Dachshunds are very clever. They were bred to think for themselves while hunting. This can make them stubborn. They are determined to follow their noses, even if it means digging under the fence to follow a scent.

BREED HISTORY

The first dachshunds lived in Germany. In the 1600s, foresters wanted short, strong dogs to hunt rabbits, foxes, badgers, and boars. The dogs had to be able to crawl through small spaces. They also had to bark loud enough when underground to let hunters know where their prey was located.

SPECIAL CONSIDERATIONS

These dogs bark a lot. If not socialized, these dogs will bark and growl at neighbors or even houseguests.

Smooth haired dachshund

GREYHOUND AKC DATE: 1885

APPEARANCE

Greyhounds are not just gray. They can be any color from white to black. They can also be red, fawn, or brown. Greyhounds can have many different patterns on their coats.

- **Height:** 26 to 30 inches (66 to 76 cm)
- **Weight:** 55 to 70 pounds (25 to 32 kg)

BEHAVIOR

Greyhounds are swift, graceful, intelligent dogs. Many greyhounds are sensitive. They get scared easily. Greyhounds do not respond well to loud noises or rough handling. Greyhounds need lots of encouragement and praise.

DID YOU KNOW?

Greyhounds can run up to 45 miles per hour (72 kmh). They are so fast because they have more muscle and less fat than most other breeds.

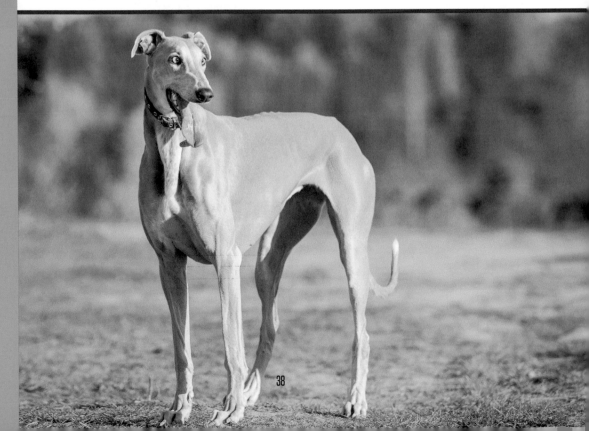

SPECIAL CONSIDERATIONS

Greyhounds do not have much fat on their bodies, so they should have soft, padded beds to prevent bedsores. They can also get hot and cold easily. It's best if they live inside.

BREED HISTORY

Greyhounds are one of the oldest dog breeds. In Egypt, tomb carvings show dogs similar to greyhounds hunting deer. Some carvings are more than 4,000 years old.

SCOTTISH DEERHOUND AKC DATE: 1886

APPEARANCE

The Scottish deerhound has a thick, shaggy-looking coat. On the body, neck, and quarters, the coat feels harsh and wiry. But on the belly, head, and chest, it feels quite soft. The coat can be a dark blue-gray, lighter gray, brindle, yellow, sandy red, or red fawn.

- **Height:** 28 to 32 inches (71 to 81 cm)
- **Weight:** 75 to 110 pounds (34 to 50 kg)

DID YOU KNOW?

Scottish deerhounds excel at coursing events. During these events, they chase a lure through an open field. Lure coursing showcases the breed's speed, agility, endurance, and ability to follow a lure.

BEHAVIOR

Scottish deerhounds are big and powerful enough to take down deer. Yet they make quiet, devoted pets. They are easy to train and have gentle temperaments.

SPECIAL CONSIDERATIONS

This breed chases small animals.

BREED HISTORY

Scottish deerhounds are one of the oldest dog breeds. They have been identified since the 1500s or 1600s. Over time, they have been called Scotch greyhounds, rough greyhounds, and highland deerhounds. They are often confused with Irish wolfhounds.

WHIPPET AKC DATE: 1888

APPEARANCE

Whippets have short, smooth coats. This breed features black, blue, fawn, red, sable, tan, and white coats. Other options are brindle or black and white. A whippet's eye color depends on its coat color. The eyes range from dark brown to nearly black.

- **Height:** 18 to 22 inches (46 to 56 cm)
- **Weight:** 25 to 40 pounds (11 to 18 kg)

BEHAVIOR

These athletic dogs are curious. That means they may run off to investigate something that catches their interest. They are quiet, gentle, and loyal and affectionate with their owners.

SPECIAL CONSIDERATIONS

Whippets have short coats. Because of this, a whippet's thin skin can be easily damaged. Owners should take special care when their whippets are running outside.

BREED HISTORY

Whippets were bred for speed, stamina, and grace. This helped them excel at chasing and capturing small game. People aren't exactly sure what breeds were used to create the whippet, but many agree that they might have some greyhound blood.

DID YOU KNOW?

Whippets are known for their speed. They can fly by at 35 miles per hour (56 kmh).

ADDITIONAL BREEDS IN THE GROUP

AFGHAN HOUND

- **What It's Known For:** Hunting
- **Where It Comes From:** Afghanistan
- **Special Considerations:** This breed likes to run and should be kept on a leash or in areas with a fence.

AMERICAN FOXHOUND

- **What It's Known For:** Hunting foxes
- **Where It Comes From:** United States
- **Special Considerations:** This breed can be destructive if it doesn't get enough exercise.

Afghan hound

Azawakh

AZAWAKH

- **What It's Known For:** Hunting and guarding
- **Where It Comes From:** West Africa
- **Special Considerations:** This breed will run and chase things.

BLACK AND TAN COONHOUND

- **What It's Known For:** Hunting
- **Where It Comes From:** United States
- **Special Considerations:** These dogs need moderate exercise every day.

Cirneco dell'Etna

CIRNECO DELL'ETNA

- **What It's Known For:** Tracking, hunting, and retrieving
- **Where It Comes From:** Italy
- **Special Considerations:** These dogs should be kept busy both mentally and physically.

GRAND BASSET GRIFFON VENDÉEN

- **What It's Known For:** Tracking
- **Where It Comes From:** France
- **Special Considerations:** This breed is curious and has a lot of energy.

Grand Basset Griffon Vendéen

ADDITIONAL BREEDS IN THE GROUP

IRISH WOLFHOUND

- **What It's Known For:** Hunting
- **Where It Comes From:** Ireland
- **Special Considerations:** These dogs are very large and can eat a lot.

Norwegian elkhound

NORWEGIAN ELKHOUND

- **What It's Known For:** Guarding and hunting
- **Where It Comes From:** Norway
- **Special Considerations:** This breed has a lot of energy and sheds.

RHODESIAN RIDGEBACK

- **What It's Known For:** Tracking
- **Where It Comes From:** Africa
- **Special Considerations:** This breed has a strong prey drive and is independent.

Rhodesian ridgeback

NONSPORTING DOGS

Dogs that don't fit well in other categories are often put in the nonsporting group. The dogs in this group can be very different from each other. They have various personalities, sizes, and colors. Standard poodles and Dalmatians are the tallest and can be 24 inches (61 cm) or more. Bichon frises are some of the smallest at around 9.5 to 11.5 inches (24 to 29 cm) tall. Dalmatians are very high energy, while bulldogs are low energy. The coats found in this group can be solid colors or patterned. The colors range from white, tan, and black to bronze, blue, and more.

Bulldog puppies

Dalmatian

BICHON FRISE AKC DATE: 1972

APPEARANCE

A bichon frise has a white, powder-puff appearance. The whole coat feels soft and silky, almost like velvet. The bichon's coat does not shed.

- **Height:** 9.5 to 11.5 inches (24 to 29 cm)
- **Weight:** 12 to 18 pounds (5 to 8 kg)

BREED HISTORY

The exact history of bichons frises is uncertain. However, it is known that four breeds of bichons originated in the Mediterranean area.

DID YOU KNOW?

A bichon frise puppy can sometimes be born with cream or apricot shadings on its coat. These colors usually disappear by the time the puppy is full grown. But sometimes an adult bichon will have cream, buff, or apricot shadings around its ears.

SPECIAL CONSIDERATIONS

Bichons frises need lots of love and attention. These dogs do not like to be left alone for long periods of time.

BEHAVIOR

Bichons frises make wonderful family pets. They are happy, playful, and intelligent. However, they will bark to warn their owners if something is wrong. Bichons frises are easy to train. They are sensitive dogs that learn quickly.

BOSTON TERRIER AKC DATE: 1893

APPEARANCE

Boston terriers have white markings on a black, brindle, or seal coat. Seal looks like black, but it has reddish tones in sunlight. Boston terriers have a single coat of smooth, short hair. This makes them easy to groom.

- **Height:** 15 to 17 inches (38 to 43 cm)
- **Weight:** The AKC recognizes three weight classes for Boston terriers. The smallest dogs weigh less than 15 pounds (7 kg). The second class is for dogs weighing 15 pounds (7 kg) to less than 20 pounds (9 kg). The final class is for Boston terriers that weigh between 20 to 25 pounds (9 to 11 kg).

BEHAVIOR

The Boston terrier is intelligent and easy to train. Their loving natures make them excellent therapy dogs. They comfort people in hospitals, nursing homes, and assisted-living homes.

DID YOU KNOW?

It is easy to recognize a Boston terrier because of its coat. The front of this dog's chest is white. This makes it look as though the dog is wearing a little tuxedo.

BREED HISTORY

The Boston terrier breed began around 1870 in Boston, Massachusetts.

BULLDOG AKC DATE: 1886

APPEARANCE

Bulldogs have smooth, short coats. They come in many colors, such as white, red, or tan. They can also be piebald. Piebald dogs are white with patches of another color. Some bulldogs are brindle.

- **Height:** 14 to 15 inches (35 to 38 cm)
- **Weight:** 40 to 50 pounds (18 to 23 kg)

DID YOU KNOW?

A bulldog's coat contains special oils that keep dirt off its body.

BEHAVIOR

Bulldogs are strong, quiet dogs. They also can be stubborn. Bulldogs are usually good around other dogs. They can enjoy the company of cats, too. But if a bulldog is not used to being around other animals, it may become protective of its toys, owner, and food.

SPECIAL CONSIDERATIONS

In hot weather, bulldogs can get overheated and have a hard time breathing.

BREED HISTORY

Bulldogs were developed hundreds of years ago in England. Early bulldogs were bred for strength and fierceness.

CHINESE SHAR-PEI AKC DATE: 1992

APPEARANCE

The Chinese shar-pei's short coat is particularly rough. This breed can either have a horse coat or brush coat. Brush coats are slightly longer and smoother. Neither coat sheds much. The most common shar-pei color is fawn. But the breed comes in a rainbow of colors. Black, cream, red, blue, and brown are just a few.

- **Height:** 18 to 20 inches (46 to 51 cm)
- **Weight:** 45 to 60 pounds (20 to 27 kg)

DID YOU KNOW?

A shar-pei's tongue and gums are often blue or black.

BEHAVIOR

The shar-pei has a calm personality. It is very loyal to its family. But this also makes it territorial and wary of strangers. Without proper socialization, the shar-pei can be quite unfriendly toward outsiders and other dogs.

SPECIAL CONSIDERATIONS

Owners should clean the dog's wrinkles often. The wrinkles can trap bacteria.

BREED HISTORY

The shar-pei breed is hundreds of years old. Archaeologists have found statues from 200 BCE that look like shar-peis. Shar-peis first worked as farm dogs in southern China. They were also popular for dogfighting. But they were more than just country dogs. Chinese royalty bred shar-peis to guard the palace and defend the royal family.

DALMATIAN AKC DATE: 1888

APPEARANCE

The Dalmatian's coat is short, dense, fine, and sleek. Black or brown spots dot the white base coat. The spots vary in size from dime sized to half-dollar sized.

- **Height:** 19 to 24 inches (48 to 61 cm)
- **Weight:** 45 to 70 pounds (20 to 32 kg)

DID YOU KNOW?

Dalmatian puppies are born pure white. Their spots begin appearing at two weeks of age.

BEHAVIOR

The Dalmatian breed is energetic and fun loving. Dalmatians are smart, even-tempered animals that love their owners.

BREED HISTORY

The Dalmatian is an old breed. Spotted dogs appear in paintings dating back to ancient Egyptian times. Because the Dalmatian goes back so far, historians are unsure where it began. However, they know the dogs once lived in Dalmatia, Croatia.

SPECIAL CONSIDERATIONS

Dalmatians can become naughty if they are not exercised. It is important to have a large, fenced-in yard for these runners.

FRENCH BULLDOG AKC DATE: 1898

APPEARANCE

French bulldogs have short, smooth coats. Their fur can be many colors including fawn, cream, or white. It can also be a combination of colors, such as brindle. The breed's famous bat ears are broad at the base, round on the top, and stand erect.

- **Height:** 11 to 13 inches (28 to 33 cm)
- **Weight:** less than 28 pounds (13 kg)

DID YOU KNOW?

It is important to take care of a French bulldog's coat. It will need occasional brushing. More frequent brushing may be needed in spring and autumn. This is when Frenchies shed.

BEHAVIOR

As companion dogs, French bulldogs are very affectionate. These intelligent dogs are alert and curious. They can be good watchdogs.

BREED HISTORY

In the late 1800s, workers in England began breeding smaller bulldogs to be lapdogs. During the Industrial Revolution (1750–1850), many English workers moved to France. They took their little bulldogs with them. In France, the bulldogs mated with other breeds. The puppies became known as French bulldogs.

SPECIAL CONSIDERATIONS

Because of the shape of its face and muzzle, a French bulldog can have difficulty breathing. So it can easily become overheated.

LHASA APSO AKC DATE: 1935

APPEARANCE

The Lhasa Apso has a thick coat that flows straight to the ground. Facial fur forms a beard and whiskers. A Lhasa Apso's coat can be any color.

- **Height:** 10 or 11 inches (25 or 28 cm)
- **Weight:** 12 to 18 pounds (5 to 8 kg)

DID YOU KNOW?

This small dog has a big-dog attitude. According to legend, when a Lhasa Apso looks in a mirror, he sees a lion. This is one reason the breed earned the nickname "little lion dog."

BEHAVIOR

Lhasa Apsos can be lively and headstrong. Training and patience can prevent bad behavior. These dogs are intelligent and are quick learners.

SPECIAL CONSIDERATIONS

Lhasa Apsos need to be groomed regularly to keep their fur shiny and tangle-free.

BREED HISTORY

Lhasa Apsos were first bred in Tibet thousands of years ago. Monks raised these dogs to be interior guards in Lhasa, Tibet's capital.

POODLE (STANDARD AND MINIATURE) AKC DATE: 1887

APPEARANCE

Poodles have thick, curly coats. Poodles come in a variety of colors. Most show poodles are either black or white. But they may also be blue, brown, silver, apricot, or cream. There are three types of poodles: toy, miniature, and standard. The toy poodle is part of the toy group. But all three poodle sizes are one breed.

- **Height:** The toy poodle is the smallest at 10 inches (25 cm) or shorter. A miniature poodle stands more than 10 inches but fewer than 15 inches (38 cm). The standard poodle is the tallest. It is more than 15 inches (38 cm) tall.
- **Weight:** 4 to 70 pounds (2 to 32 kg)

Standard poodle

SPECIAL CONSIDERATIONS

Poodles are bred to be around people. They crave love and attention. Exercise is also important for this breed.

BEHAVIOR

This graceful dog is very intelligent. It can easily learn new tricks and commands. Poodles make great family pets. Miniature and standard poodles in particular are good with children.

DID YOU KNOW?

One bonus for many owners is that the poodle's coat doesn't shed. But it does require a lot of work. Poodles need regular brushing and professional grooming. Brushing alone can take a couple of hours each week. And grooming can get expensive.

BREED HISTORY

The poodle breed began in Germany. The first poodles were water dogs. Hunters used them to retrieve ducks and geese from water during a hunt.

XOLOITZCUINTLI AKC DATE: 2011

APPEARANCE

The Xoloitzcuintli, or Xolo for short, is best known for its hairless body. However, there are both hairless and coated Xolos. Both types come in many colors. They range from black to red to bronze. The Xolo comes in three sizes. They are toy, miniature, and standard.

- **Height:** Toy Xolos stand 10 to 14 inches (25 to 36 cm) at the shoulder. Miniature Xolos range from 14 to 18 inches (36 to 46 cm). The standard Xolo runs from 18 to 23 inches (46 to 58 cm) tall.
- **Weight:** 10 to 55 pounds (4.5 to 25 kg)

BEHAVIOR

The adult Xolo is calm and attentive to its family. The Xolo is a social breed. Its intelligence helps it to retain information and train well. The Xolo is alert and territorial. It is an excellent guard dog.

DID YOU KNOW?

The hairless Xolo's skin is smooth, tough, and fits snugly to the body. The lack of hair exposes the Xolo to sunlight and the cold. So they need sunscreen in the summer and a sweater in the colder months.

BREED HISTORY

Artifacts found in Mexico show the Xolo has been there nearly 3,500 years. The Xolo is one of the world's oldest breeds.

SPECIAL CONSIDERATIONS

The Xolo is an active dog. It needs a large area in which to run and play. Climbing over a 6-foot (2-m) fence is no problem for this athletic breed.

ADDITIONAL BREEDS IN THE GROUP

AMERICAN ESKIMO DOG

- **What It's Known For:** Sled dog
- **Where It Comes From:** Germany
- **Special Considerations:** This breed is very intelligent.

CHOW CHOW

- **What It's Known For:** Guarding and hunting
- **Where It Comes From:** China
- **Special Considerations:** Without proper socialization, Chow Chows can be aggressive.

American Eskimo Dog

COTON DE TULEAR

- **What It's Known For:** Companionship
- **Where It Comes From:** Madagascar
- **Special Considerations:** This breed has a lot of fur, so these dogs must be groomed.

Chow Chow

Finnish spitz

FINNISH SPITZ

- **What It's Known For:** Tracking
- **Where It Comes From:** Finland
- **Special Considerations:** This breed is intelligent and can sometimes be hard to train.

KEESHOND

- **What It's Known For:** Friendly and happy attitude
- **Where It Comes From:** Holland
- **Special Considerations:** This breed should be groomed regularly.

Keeshond

ADDITIONAL BREEDS IN THE GROUP

LÖWCHEN

- **What It's Known For:** Companionship
- **Where It Comes From:** France and Germany
- **Special Considerations:** This breed can bark a lot.

NORWEGIAN LUNDEHUND

- **What It's Known For:** Hunting and companionship
- **Where It Comes From:** Norway
- **Special Considerations:** This breed is energetic and needs regular exercise.

Löwchen

SHIBA INU

- **What It's Known For:** Hunting and companionship
- **Where It Comes From:** Japan
- **Special Considerations:** This breed is independent and is known to escape.

TIBETAN SPANIEL

- **What It's Known For:** Companionship
- **Where It Comes From:** Tibet
- **Special Considerations:** This breed is independent.

Shiba Inu

Tibetan spaniel

SPORTING DOGS

Dogs in the sporting group have historically been used for hunting. With training, these dogs can find animals, drive them from their hiding spots, and then retrieve them once hunters have shot them down. Sporting dogs are known to be trainable and gentle with people. They are great family dogs.

Irish setter

Golden retriever

BRITTANY AKC DATE: 1934

APPEARANCE

A Brittany's coat has fine, flat hair. The hair can be straight or wavy. A Brittany's coat may be orange and white, liver and white, or black and white.

- **Height:** 17.5 to 20.5 inches (44 to 52 cm)
- **Weight:** 30 to 40 pounds (14 to 18 kg)

DID YOU KNOW?

Brittanys are one of Europe's oldest hunting breeds.

BEHAVIOR

Brittanys have incredible tracking and retrieving skills. Brittanys are excellent pets for an active family. They are gentle, loving, and intelligent.

SPECIAL CONSIDERATIONS

Brittanys should be treated gently. Otherwise they may become timid and shy.

BREED HISTORY

Brittanys were first bred in the 1800s. They received their name from the area they originated from: Brittany, France.

COCKER SPANIEL AKC DATE: 1878

APPEARANCE

The cocker spaniel has a long, soft, silky coat. The coat can be flat or wavy. Cockers come in a variety of colors. They can be solid black or black with tan markings. They can also be any solid color from light cream to dark red.

- **Height:** 14.5 to 15.5 inches (37 to 39 cm)
- **Weight:** 20 to 30 pounds (9 to 14 kg)

BEHAVIOR

Cocker spaniels are playful, loving, friendly dogs. As hunters, cockers have good senses of hearing and smell.

BREED HISTORY

This breed's roots date back to at least the 1300s. Historians believe spaniels came from Spain. Humans bred them to be hunting dogs. The smallest of the spaniel breeds is the cocker spaniel. This dog is named for its ability to hunt birds called woodcocks.

DID YOU KNOW?

Some cockers have parti-color coats. These coats display two or more solid colors. A parti-color cocker may be black and white, red and white, or brown and white.

SPECIAL CONSIDERATIONS

These dogs require regular grooming. This will keep their coats from becoming matted and tangled.

GOLDEN RETRIEVER AKC DATE: 1925

APPEARANCE

Golden retrievers have beautiful double coats. The golden's undercoat is a light cream color. The outercoat is a darker shade of gold.

- **Height:** 21.5 to 24 inches (55 to 61 cm)
- **Weight:** 55 to 75 pounds (25 to 34 kg)

DID YOU KNOW?

Golden retrievers do not make good guard dogs. They may bark at strangers, but they will quickly warm up to them.

BEHAVIOR

Golden retrievers are sensitive, loving dogs. They want to be with their people, including children. They are good with other dogs, too. These dogs need an owner who is able to train them and give them attention.

BREED HISTORY

In the 1800s, an English sportsman named Dudley Marjoribanks bred many animals. One day, he met a man who had a golden-coated retriever that had been born in a litter of black puppies. Marjoribanks bred that dog, and over time the golden retriever was developed.

SPECIAL CONSIDERATIONS

Goldens are energetic. They need exercise every day. If they don't get enough exercise, they can get into trouble. This can include a lot of unwanted chewing.

IRISH RED AND WHITE SETTER AKC DATE: 2009

APPEARANCE

An Irish red and white setter has a white coat with chestnut-red patches. Most of this breed's coat is of medium length and either flat or wavy.

- **Height:** 22.5 to 26 inches (57 to 66 cm)
- **Weight:** 35 to 60 pounds (16 to 27 kg)

BEHAVIOR

Irish red and white setters need a lot of attention. They are friendly dogs that usually get along well with people. This spirited breed is also very smart.

DID YOU KNOW?

These dogs are happier and easier to live with if they know the rules and know who's the boss. Training may require more time with this breed than other hunting dogs.

BREED HISTORY

Long ago in Ireland, hunters depended on dogs to help them hunt. By the late 1600s, setters were a popular choice. Some setters were all red. Others were red and white. Eventually, these different-colored dogs became known as two separate breeds. They are the Irish setter and the Irish red and white setter.

SPECIAL CONSIDERATIONS

Longer fur can easily become tangled or matted. Owners may need to groom their Irish red and white setters daily.

IRISH SETTER AKC DATE: 1878

APPEARANCE

The Irish setter's coat is medium length. A healthy coat is silky and shiny. An Irish setter's coat can range in color from chestnut red to deep mahogany.

- **Height:** 25 to 27 inches (64 to 69 cm)
- **Weight:** 60 to 70 pounds (27 to 32 kg)

DID YOU KNOW?

Irish setters develop more slowly than other dog breeds. They do not fully develop until they are two to three years old.

BEHAVIOR

Irish setters are highly active and need regular exercise. They are strong, intelligent, and fun-loving dogs.

BREED HISTORY

Irish setters were first bred in Ireland in the 1800s. They are probably a combination of several breeds. These breeds may include English setters, Gordon setters, and pointers.

SPECIAL CONSIDERATIONS

Exercise is a must for an Irish setter. Lack of exercise can cause an Irish setter to misbehave.

LABRADOR RETRIEVER AKC DATE: 1917

APPEARANCE

The Labrador retriever has a short, straight, dense coat. This popular breed comes in three colors. These are black, yellow, and chocolate.

- **Height:** 21.5 to 24.5 inches (55 to 62 cm)
- **Weight:** 55 to 80 pounds (25 to 36 kg)

DID YOU KNOW?

Labs can serve as military dogs, police dogs, and guide dogs. These dogs are also useful in disasters. Labs commonly help search and rescue teams.

BREED HISTORY

The Labrador retriever breed is from
Newfoundland and Labrador in Canada.
There, it helped fishermen haul in nets
and catch escaping fish.

BEHAVIOR

Labs are even-tempered, smart, strong, and healthy. Labs also love
to play. They especially enjoy water. These lively dogs are highly
trainable. However, they do not make the best guard dogs.

POINTER AKC DATE: 1878

APPEARANCE

The pointer has a short, compact coat. The fur is smooth with a sheen. The pointer's coat comes in four colors. These are black, liver, lemon, and orange. The coat can be either one solid color or a color combined with white.

- **Height:** 23 to 28 inches (58 to 71 cm)
- **Weight:** 45 to 75 pounds (20 to 34 kg)

DID YOU KNOW?

Even after hunting, this breed usually just needs a quick brushing to get rid of burrs and debris.

BEHAVIOR

Pointers are loyal and devoted, so they make wonderful family pets. They are smart dogs that are eager to please. They learn quickly with positive obedience training.

SPECIAL CONSIDERATIONS

Pointers require daily exercise. Also, this breed needs a fenced-in yard.

BREED HISTORY

Pointers appeared in Spain, Portugal, eastern Europe, and the British Isles around the same time. They were first recorded in England around 1650. For this reason, they are sometimes called English pointers. Pointers are a mixture of the bloodhound, the greyhound, and foxhound breeds.

SPRINGER SPANIEL AKC DATE: 1910 (ENGLISH); 1914 (WELSH)

APPEARANCE

There are English springer spaniels and Welsh springer spaniels. The English springer spaniel's medium-length outercoat can be flat or wavy. The Welsh springer spaniel has a straight, soft, flat coat. The English coat comes in a variety of colors, such as liver, black, or reddish brown with white markings. The Welsh coat does not have as much variety. It is rich red and white only.

English springer spaniel
- **Height:** 19 to 20 inches (48 to 51 cm)
- **Weight:** 40 to 50 pounds (18 to 23 kg)

Welsh springer spaniel
- **Height:** 17 to 19 inches (43 to 48 cm)
- **Weight:** 35 to 55 pounds (16 to 25 kg)

DID YOU KNOW?

Originally, the Welsh breed hunted along the coastlines of Wales, Ireland, and Scotland. They became the favorite hunting dogs of nobles.

English springer spaniel

Welsh springer spaniel

BEHAVIOR

Friendly and affectionate, springer spaniels make cheerful playmates. Springer spaniels quickly learn commands. Positive obedience training can make lessons fun.

BREED HISTORY

In the past, both springer spaniels and cocker spaniels appeared in the same litters. Littermates weighing more than 28 pounds (13 kg) were labeled springers.

English springer spaniel puppy

WEIMARANER AKC DATE: 1943

APPEARANCE

Weimaraners have a short, smooth, sleek gray coat. The shades of gray can range from blue-gray to silver-gray.

- **Height:** 23 to 27 inches (58 to 69 cm)
- **Weight:** 55 to 90 pounds (25 to 41 kg)

DID YOU KNOW?

Some Weimaraners have long hair. Long- and short-haired Weimaraner puppies can be born in the same litter. Fans of the long-haired coat tried to get the AKC to recognize these types of Weimaraners. That effort failed.

BEHAVIOR

Weimaraners are fearless, friendly, obedient, and alert. The dogs are so smart that some have become service dogs. They assist people with disabilities. Others have served as rescue dogs.

SPECIAL CONSIDERATIONS

If a Weimaraner does not have a fenced-in yard, it may wander off looking for something to hunt.

BREED HISTORY

The Weimaraner is a relatively young breed. It dates back to the early 1800s. The dogs were first known as Weimar pointers. They were named after Weimar, an area in what is now Germany.

ADDITIONAL BREEDS IN THE GROUP

AMERICAN WATER SPANIEL

- **What It's Known For:** Scaring game out of hiding places and retrieving
- **Where It Comes From:** United States
- **Special Considerations:** This dog needs to be groomed weekly.

CHESAPEAKE BAY RETRIEVER

- **What It's Known For:** Retrieving
- **Where It Comes From:** United States
- **Special Considerations:** This breed is high energy and requires lots of exercise.

Chesapeake Bay retriever

Clumber spaniel

CLUMBER SPANIEL

- **What It's Known For:** Scaring and retrieving game out of hiding places
- **Where It Comes From:** Unknown
- **Special Considerations:** Because of the breed's body shape, it's important that these dogs don't get overweight.

GORDON SETTER

- **What It's Known For:** Bird dog
- **Where It Comes From:** Scotland
- **Special Considerations:** This dog should have the thick hair between its toes trimmed so its feet stay healthy.

LAGOTTO ROMAGNOLO

- **What It's Known For:** Retrieving waterfowl and finding truffles.
- **Where It Comes From:** Italy
- **Special Considerations:** Some dogs in this breed can get matted coats, so regular grooming is essential.

Gordon setter

ADDITIONAL BREEDS IN THE GROUP

NEDERLANDSE KOOIKERHONDJE

- **What It's Known For:**
  Luring ducks
- **Where It Comes From:**
  Netherlands
- **Special Considerations:** This breed loves attention from its humans but can be wary of strangers.

NOVA SCOTIA DUCK TOLLING RETRIEVER

- **What It's Known For:** Luring ducks from the water and retrieving
- **Where It Comes From:** Nova Scotia
- **Special Considerations:** This breed needs a lot of exercise.

Nederlandse kooikerhondje

Nova Scotia duck tolling retriever

Vizsla

SPINONE ITALIANO

- **What It's Known For:** Finding and retrieving game
- **Where It Comes From:** Italy
- **Special Considerations:** Some dogs in this breed can get bloat.

VIZSLA

- **What It's Known For:** Hunting
- **Where It Comes From:** Hungary
- **Special Considerations:** This breed needs mental and physical exercise.

TERRIER DOGS

The terrier group has many dogs with feisty personalities. These breeds were developed to both hunt and kill rodents and other vermin. Some terriers even hunt foxes. Dogs in the group can range in size. They also have many different kinds of coats. Some have short, smooth coats and others have long, wiry fur.

Airedale terrier

Russell terrier

AIREDALE TERRIER AKC DATE: 1888

APPEARANCE

The Airedale terrier has a dense coat that is resistant to dampness. The coat's hard, wiry outer hair lies close to the body and can be a bit wavy. Underneath this stiff hair is another layer of shorter, softer hair.

- **Height:** 23 inches (58 cm)
- **Weight:** 50 to 70 pounds (23 to 32 kg)

DID YOU KNOW?

Airedale terriers were originally bred for hunting foxes, otters, and badgers. During World War I (1914–1918), Airedales worked as guard dogs and messengers for the British army. Today, Airedale terriers are common family pets.

BEHAVIOR

Airedale terriers make excellent pets. They are intelligent, affectionate, energetic, and easy to train. Airedales can also be stubborn at times, but they are loyal to their owners.

BREED HISTORY

Airedales were developed in the 1800s in Yorkshire, England. They were named for the Aire River in Yorkshire.

SPECIAL CONSIDERATIONS

Airedales, like other terriers, have lots of energy. They need exercise every day. Also, their coats need regular grooming.

AMERICAN STAFFORDSHIRE TERRIER

AKC DATE: 1936

APPEARANCE

American Staffordshire terriers have a broad head with a distinct jaw. These dogs have a muscular build, and their coats can range in color. They can be black, blue, bronze, fawn, liver, red, white, and a variety of brindle or sable colors.

- **Height:** 17 to 19 inches (43 to 48 cm)
- **Weight:** 40 to 70 pounds (18 to 32 kg)

DID YOU KNOW?

An American Staffordshire terrier is considered one of the greatest war dogs. His name was Sergeant Stubby, and he served in World War I. He helped soldiers on the battlefield, and it is rumored that he could smell out poisonous gas.

BEHAVIOR

American Staffordshire terriers are intelligent, courageous, and loyal. These dogs like to be challenged both mentally and physically.

SPECIAL CONSIDERATIONS

This breed likes to dig and chew.

BREED HISTORY

Staffordshire terriers were developed in England. In the mid-1800s, these dogs came to the United States. People began breeding them to be larger than the English terriers and created the American Staffordshire terrier.

BULL TERRIER AKC DATE: 1885

APPEARANCE

The bull terrier has a short, flat, glossy coat. The bull terrier's coat comes in two varieties. They are white and colored. White bullies can have a spot of color on their heads. But their bodies are all white. Colored bull terriers can be black and tan, brindle, red, or fawn.

- **Height:** 21 to 22 inches (53 to 56 cm)
- **Weight:** 50 to 70 pounds (23 to 32 kg)

DID YOU KNOW?

Bullies will sometimes "talk" with groans and grunts. However, they do not bark very often.

BEHAVIOR

Bullies are lively and playful. They love to stay busy and should have toys to keep them occupied. These affectionate dogs are very devoted to family. If kept apart, they are not happy. Bullies love to be close to their people.

SPECIAL CONSIDERATIONS

Bull terriers can develop several health problems. Kidney, heart, and skin problems are common in this breed.

BREED HISTORY

In the 1860s, James Hinks of Birmingham, England, crossed the bull-and-terrier with the Dalmatian, the bulldog, and the white English terrier. In this way, Hinks created the bull terrier.

CESKY TERRIER AKC DATE: 2011

APPEARANCE

The Cesky terrier's coat is soft and slightly wavy. Individual hairs are fine but firm. Cesky terriers come in two color varieties. Light brown Ceskies are born chocolate brown. Gray-blue Ceskies are far more common. They are born black. As adults, they come in a range of shades of gray.

- **Height:** 10 to 13 inches (25 to 33 cm)
- **Weight:** 14 to 24 pounds (6 to 11 kg)

DID YOU KNOW?

The Cesky's unique hairstyle is one of its most recognizable features. The standard cut consists of very short hair on the ears, cheeks, tail, and upper torso. Long hair forms the breed's distinctive beard and hangs over its face. More long, wavy hair flowing from the legs and belly completes the look.

BEHAVIOR

Cesky terriers are highly active and need regular exercise. Ceskies are also loving family dogs. This loyal breed is protective of its family.

BREED HISTORY

The Cesky terrier originated in what is now the Czech Republic. It came about by breeding a Scottish terrier with a Sealyham terrier in 1949.

SPECIAL CONSIDERATIONS

The Cesky's hairstyle requires monthly clipping. Also, frequent brushing removes and prevents mats.

MINIATURE SCHNAUZER AKC DATE: 1926

APPEARANCE

The miniature schnauzer has a double coat. The outercoat is harsh and wiry. It protects a short, thick undercoat. These dogs can be different colors, including solid black, salt-and-pepper, and black and silver.

- **Height:** 12 to 14 inches (30 to 36 cm)
- **Weight:** 11 to 20 pounds (5 to 9 kg)

DID YOU KNOW?

Owners can influence the look of a miniature schnauzer. Some crop the ears, which gives the ears pointed tips. Uncropped ears are small and fold over in the shape of a *V*. The miniature schnauzer's docked tail is set high and carried upright.

BEHAVIOR

The miniature schnauzer is a small, spunky dog. Miniature schnauzers display great intelligence. They are very successful in obedience classes. This is because they are eager to please, and they train easily.

SPECIAL CONSIDERATIONS

This breed has an independent streak. Miniature schnauzers who become bored may bark and seek out their own amusements.

BREED HISTORY

Paintings of schnauzer dogs date back to the 1400s. This breed developed in Germany. The first schnauzers were bred by crossing black poodles and gray wolf spitzes with wirehaired pinschers. The miniature schnauzer was bred by crossing standard schnauzers, poodles, and affenpinschers.

RAT TERRIER AKC DATE: 2013

APPEARANCE

The rat terrier, or ratty, has a short, dense, and smooth coat. The breed comes in many colors, including blue, lemon, and chocolate. The AKC recognizes standard and miniature sized ratties that can be between 10 to 25 pounds (4.5 to 11 kg).

Standard ratties
- **Height:** 13 to 18 inches (33 to 46 cm)

Miniature ratties
- **Height:** 10 to 13 inches (25 to 33 cm)

DID YOU KNOW?

Some people say President Theodore Roosevelt gave the rat terrier its name. Roosevelt had two, and he named the breed this because the dogs cleared the White House of rats.

BEHAVIOR

The ratty is playful, active, and curious. However, this breed is territorial and suspicious of strangers. And the rat terrier has a strong prey drive. It does not do well with smaller animals.

SPECIAL CONSIDERATIONS

The rat terrier's jumping and digging skills make it a true escape artist. So a high fence and watchful eye are essential.

BREED HISTORY

The rat terrier has been called a "breed of many breeds." Its ancestor, the feist, was a mix of many different terriers. Breeders began crossing the feist with other dogs. Eventually, this led to the rat terrier.

RUSSELL TERRIER AKC DATE: 2012

APPEARANCE

A Russell terrier's coat can either be rough, smooth, or broken. A rough coat has the longest fur. The fur is wiry. A smooth coat has short, thick hairs that are flat against the dog's body. A broken coat is in between rough and smooth length, with some wiry hairs on the face. All coat types have a short undercoat. Russell terriers are mostly white, with black or tan markings on their bodies.

- **Height:** 10 to 12 inches (25 to 30 cm)
- **Weight:** 9 to 15 pounds (4 to 7 kg)

DID YOU KNOW?

Russell terriers need lots of love and attention. Mostly, they need lots of exercise. A Russell terrier that gets the right amount of exercise will be less likely to go off on its own and get into trouble.

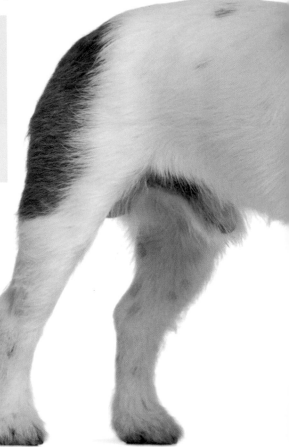

BEHAVIOR

Russell terriers are very active dogs. Most are not afraid of anything. They are very smart and will obey their owners if they are trained properly.

BREED HISTORY

The Russell terrier was developed in the 1800s in England.

SPECIAL CONSIDERATIONS

Russell terriers are sometimes not very good with other dogs because they like to fight.

SCOTTISH TERRIER AKC DATE: 1885

APPEARANCE

Scottish terriers, or Scotties, have a thick, wiry coat that is kept short on their backs and grows longer on their sides, like a skirt. Scotties are black, brindle, or a cream color.

- **Height:** 10 inches (25 cm)
- **Weight:** 18 to 22 pounds (8 to 10 kg)

DID YOU KNOW?

This terrier is persistent and has been nicknamed the "diehard."

BEHAVIOR

Scotties are playful and active, and they are protective of their humans. They make good watchdogs. The Scottie can be independent. They are good with children who treat them kindly. Scotties may snap at children who tease them.

BREED HISTORY

The Scottie originally came from Aberdeen, Scotland.

SPECIAL CONSIDERATIONS

The Scottie's coat needs to be combed three times a week. The Scottie's eyes, ears, teeth, and nails should be checked regularly to make sure they are healthy.

WEST HIGHLAND WHITE TERRIER
AKC DATE: 1908

APPEARANCE

The West Highland white terrier is known for its solid white coat.

- **Height:** 10 to 11 inches (25 to 28 cm)
- **Weight:** 15 to 20 pounds (7 to 9 kg)

DID YOU KNOW?

In the past, the terrier's main job was to control the population of rats and other vermin. They dove right into animal holes to capture their prey. Fox hunters also valued these hardy dogs.

BEHAVIOR

The West Highland white terrier is a hardworking breed that is energetic and loves to dig. The Westie can also be a barker. It was bred this way so it could be found even when chasing prey underground. With proper training, the Westie can learn to bark only when appropriate.

SPECIAL CONSIDERATIONS

A long daily walk or a run outdoors keeps this dog happy and fit.

BREED HISTORY

The West Highland white terrier originated in Scotland.

ADDITIONAL BREEDS IN THE GROUP

AMERICAN HAIRLESS TERRIER

- **What It's Known For:** Hunting vermin
- **Where It Comes From:** United States
- **Special Considerations:** American Hairless terriers without fur can get sunburn and need extra protection when it's cold outside.

American hairless terrier

AUSTRALIAN TERRIER

- **What It's Known For:** Hunting small critters
- **Where It Comes From:** Australia
- **Special Considerations:** Australian terriers like to chase small animals and enjoy digging.

BEDLINGTON TERRIER

- **What It's Known For:** Hunting and companionship
- **Where It Comes From:** England
- **Special Considerations:** The Bedlington terrier's coat should be clipped about every two months.

Australian Terrier

CAIRN TERRIER

- **What It's Known For:** Finding small prey
- **Where It Comes From:** Scotland
- **Special Considerations:** This breed has a high prey drive and will dig holes.

DANDIE DINMONT TERRIER

- **What It's Known For:** Hunting badgers and otters
- **Where It Comes From:** The border of England and Scotland
- **Special Considerations:** This breed needs to be brushed every day.

Cairn terrier

Dandie Dinmont terrier

ADDITIONAL BREEDS IN THE GROUP

KERRY BLUE TERRIER

- **What It's Known For:** Hunting small animals and retrieving
- **Where It Comes From:** Ireland
- **Special Considerations:** This breed can be stubborn.

PARSON RUSSELL TERRIER

- **What It's Known For:** Fox hunting
- **Where It Comes From:** England
- **Special Considerations:** This breed has lots of energy.

Kerry blue terrier

SEALYHAM TERRIER

- **What It's Known For:** Hunting otters, badgers, and foxes
- **Where It Comes From:** Wales
- **Special Considerations:** This breed's coat has been known to mat, so it needs regular brushing.

Sealyham terrier

WELSH TERRIER

- **What It's Known For:** Hunting otters, badgers, and other small game
- **Where It Comes From:** Wales
- **Special Considerations:** This breed has lots of energy and likes to play with people.

WIRE FOX TERRIER

- **What It's Known For:** Hunting
- **Where It Comes From:** England
- **Special Considerations:** These dogs need to be brushed often so their coats don't mat.

Wire fox terrier

115

TOY DOGS

Dogs in the toy group offer companionship to people and are good options for those who have a small living space. Some dogs in this group look like mini versions of larger dog breeds, such as the toy poodle or miniature pinscher. Dogs in this group are usually small. They can range from less than 6 pounds (3 kg) to around 20 pounds (9 kg). These dogs might bark a lot, but they are seen as easier to physically control because of their sizes.

Cavalier King Charles spaniel

Pomeranian

AFFENPINSCHER AKC DATE: 1936

APPEARANCE

The affenpinscher's coat is shaggy but neat. It comes in a variety of colors, such as black, gray, silver, red, and black and tan.

- **Height:** 9 to 11.5 inches (23 to 29 cm)
- **Weight:** 7 to 10 pounds (3 to 4.5 kg)

BEHAVIOR

The affenpinscher is territorial, independent, and bold. These qualities make the affenpinscher an excellent watchdog. In addition, the affenpinscher has not lost its natural hunting instinct. So keep hamsters, gerbils, and other rodent-like pets safe around this breed.

BREED HISTORY

The affenpinscher originated in central Europe.

DID YOU KNOW?

The name "monkey terrier" describes the affenpinscher's looks and many of its behaviors. For instance, this dog has a tendency to walk on its back legs, which makes some people think that it looks like a monkey.

SPECIAL CONSIDERATIONS

With its short muzzle, this breed can easily become overheated. And some affenpinschers can have joint and vision problems.

CAVALIER KING CHARLES SPANIEL
AKC DATE: 1995

APPEARANCE

Cavalier King Charles spaniels have long, silky, flowing coats. They come in different colors including ruby, black and white, and black and tan.

- **Height:** 12 to 13 inches (30 to 33 cm)
- **Weight:** 13 to 18 pounds (6 to 8 kg)

DID YOU KNOW?

Cavalier King Charles spaniels are very adaptable. They will fit their activity levels based on how active their humans are.

BEHAVIOR

Cavalier King Charles spaniels are gentle, playful dogs. Cavaliers do not need much exercise. Cavaliers were bred to be companion dogs. As long as they spend most of the time with their owners, Cavaliers are happy.

BREED HISTORY

For centuries, toy spaniels were popular with England's aristocracy. King Charles II had lots of toy spaniels. Many years later, breeders worked to produce dogs that looked like King Charles's.

CHIHUAHUA AKC DATE: 1904

APPEARANCE

Chihuahuas can have one of two different kinds of coats. Some have smooth coats, which are short, soft, and look glossy. Other Chihuahuas have long coats, which are very soft and can be straight or a little curly. Chihuahuas can be a number of different colors, from sandy white to blue or even black.

- **Height:** 5 to 8 inches (13 to 20 cm)
- **Weight:** less than 6 pounds (2.7 kg)

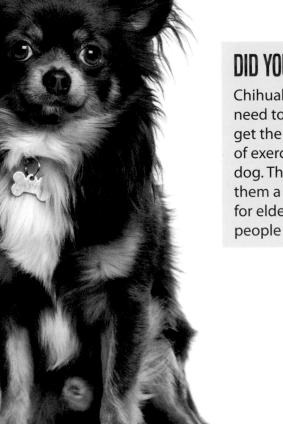

DID YOU KNOW?

Chihuahuas don't need to walk as far to get the same amount of exercise as a larger dog. That can make them a good choice for elderly people or people in cities.

BEHAVIOR

Chihuahuas are happy little dogs. They are very smart and they learn quickly. They love to be with their owners and other Chihuahuas, but they are shy around other breeds of dogs. They also are nervous around strangers.

BREED HISTORY

The Chihuahua got its name because the modern breed was discovered in 1850 in Chihuahua, Mexico.

SPECIAL CONSIDERATIONS

Chihuahuas should not be left outside in weather that is very hot or cold. They also need regular cleaning of their ears and teeth.

MALTESE AKC DATE: 1888

APPEARANCE

Maltese have a soft, snow-white coat that is long and straight. It flows right to the ground.

- **Height:** 7 to 9 inches (18 to 23 cm)
- **Weight:** less than 7 pounds (3 kg)

BEHAVIOR

Maltese crave attention. They are eager to play, and they quickly make new friends. Despite their small size, Maltese are fearless and spirited. They usually bark at strangers. So they make good watchdogs.

DID YOU KNOW?

In the 1600s and 1700s, Maltese could snuggle in a lady's sleeve. A woman in the 1800s would sometimes match her pet's hair ribbons to the color of her dress.

BREED HISTORY

The Maltese breed dates back more than 2,800 years. These dogs were first brought to the Mediterranean island of Malta around this time. Malta was a trading center between Africa and Europe.

SPECIAL CONSIDERATIONS

Maltese need daily brushing. They also need a bath at least once every month to keep their silky coats gleaming.

POMERANIAN AKC DATE: 1888

APPEARANCE

Pomeranians, or Poms, have a variety of coat colors. Orange and red are the most popular. Brown, cream, black, and blue are other common colors.

- **Height:** 6 to 7 inches (15 to 18 cm)
- **Weight:** 3 to 7 pounds (1.4 to 3 kg)

BEHAVIOR

This happy, intelligent breed loves to be with its family. It enjoys playing games, learning new tricks, and taking walks. They are loyal to their owners and protective of their homes.

BREED HISTORY

The name *Pomeranian* was first used by Queen Charlotte of England. In 1761, she got dogs from Pomerania and named them for the area. Today, this area is part of Germany and Poland.

SPECIAL CONSIDERATIONS

The Pom's fluffy double coat sheds all year long. Owners need to groom their dogs often. This will prevent the coat from getting tangled or matted.

PUG AKC DATE: 1885

APPEARANCE

A pug's coat is made up of short, thin fur that is very soft and smooth. The pug's face and ears are black, and its body can be black or fawn.

- **Height:** 10 to 13 inches (25 to 33 cm)
- **Weight:** 14 to 18 pounds (6 to 8 kg)

BEHAVIOR

Pugs are happy little dogs that love to be in the middle of the action. They are very friendly and love to play with people. Pugs are smart and easy to train.

DID YOU KNOW?

Pugs tend to snore.

BREED HISTORY

The pug is one of the oldest breeds of dogs. It started in China and Tibet more than 2,400 years ago.

SPECIAL CONSIDERATIONS

A pug's wrinkles need to be cleaned daily. In addition, because of their pushed-in faces, pugs sometimes have breathing problems, especially in hot weather.

SHIH TZU AKC DATE: 1969

APPEARANCE

Shih Tzus have thick, long, and flowy coats. They can be in any color, from white to black. Most Shih Tzus have more than one color in their fur.

- **Height:** 9 to 10.5 inches (23 to 27 cm)
- **Weight:** 9 to 16 pounds (4 to 7 kg)

BEHAVIOR

Shih Tzus love to play with people and to have their long coats brushed. Even though they are small, they make good watchdogs. They have a lot of courage, and they will bark at things out of the ordinary.

DID YOU KNOW?

Shih Tzus don't need as much exercise as larger dogs, but they do need to be taken on walks. A good game of fetch, indoors or out, will help keep a Shih Tzu healthy.

BREED HISTORY

Shih Tzu is a Chinese word that means "lion" or "lion dog." They first became popular dogs in China in the 600s. They became a favorite dog of Chinese royalty, and many sculptures and paintings in China included a Shih Tzu.

SPECIAL CONSIDERATIONS

Shih Tzus need daily grooming in order to avoid a matted coat. Their eyes, teeth, and ears should be checked often.

YORKSHIRE TERRIER AKC DATE: 1885

APPEARANCE

Yorkshire terriers, or Yorkies, have beautiful coats that can be blue and tan or black and tan.

- **Height:** 7 to 8 inches (18 to 20 cm)
- **Weight:** 7 pounds (3 kg)

BEHAVIOR

Yorkshire terriers can be wonderful lap dogs. But they have terrier traits that make them independent, stubborn, and fierce. They are confident and alert, and they have a strong will.

DID YOU KNOW?

Yorkies can be very demanding. They want all of your attention all of the time. They don't want to be alone.

BREED HISTORY

In the mid-1800s, the Yorkshire terrier was bred in Lancashire and Yorkshire, England.

SPECIAL CONSIDERATIONS

Yorkies should not be exposed to extreme weather conditions.

ADDITIONAL BREEDS IN THE GROUP

BRUSSELS GRIFFON

- **What It's Known For:** Companionship
- **Where It Comes From:** Belgium
- **Special Considerations:** This breed is sensitive and needs positive interactions.

CHINESE CRESTED

- **What It's Known For:** Companionship
- **Where It Comes From:** China
- **Special Considerations:** The hairless crested can get sunburn and skin irritations. The coated crested should be brushed every day.

Brussels griffon

Chinese crested

ENGLISH TOY SPANIEL

- **What It's Known For:** Companionship
- **Where It Comes From:** Unknown
- **Special Considerations:** This breed can be stubborn.

HAVANESE

- **What It's Known For:** Companionship
- **Where It Comes From:** Cuba
- **Special Considerations:** This breed can be sensitive.

ITALIAN GREYHOUND

- **What It's Known For:** Companionship
- **Where It Comes From:** Italy
- **Special Considerations:** These dogs will quickly run after prey. They also need protection when it's cold outside.

Japanese chin

PAPILLON

- **What It's Known For:** Companionship
- **Where It Comes From:** Spain and Italy
- **Special Considerations:** Because these dogs are so small, people should be careful when handling them.

PEKINGESE

- **What It's Known For:** Companionship
- **Where It Comes From:** China
- **Special Considerations:** This breed can be stubborn.

JAPANESE CHIN

- **What It's Known For:** Companionship
- **Where It Comes From:** Unknown
- **Special Considerations:** A Japanese Chin's nails grow quickly and need to be trimmed often. Its ears and teeth also need to be checked.

MINIATURE PINSCHER

- **What It's Known For:** Companionship
- **Where It Comes From:** Unknown, but some say it could be from Germany.
- **Special Considerations:** This breed needs exercise regularly. It is also independent.

Pekingese

WORKING DOGS

Dogs in the working group have been bred to do various jobs. These include pulling sleds, guarding both property and livestock, and participating in water rescues. These dogs are smart and learn fast. They are also very strong and need to be appropriately trained.

Siberian huskies

Greater Swiss mountain dog

ALASKAN MALAMUTE AKC DATE: 1935

APPEARANCE

The Alaskan malamute's coat and natural oils keep out water and the cold. These dogs have face and body markings that range in color, such as black and white, blue and white, red and white, and silver and white.

- **Height:** 23 to 25 inches (58 to 64 cm)
- **Weight:** 75 to 85 pounds (34 to 39 kg)

DID YOU KNOW?

Malamutes can survive at temperatures as low as -70 degrees Fahrenheit (-60°C).

BEHAVIOR

The Alaskan malamute is a playful, affectionate dog. But owners must know how to master the malamute's independent nature. If not kept in their place, these strong-willed dogs will attempt to run the household.

BREED HISTORY

The Alaskan malamute was developed in the 1800s by the Mahlemut people in northwest Alaska. Now known as the Kuuvangmiut, they settled on the Kotzebue Sound in the upper-western part of what is now Alaska.

SPECIAL CONSIDERATIONS

The athletic Alaskan malamute has a great need for activity and exercise. Malamutes without enough exercise become bored and destructive.

BERNESE MOUNTAIN DOG AKC DATE: 1937

APPEARANCE

Bernese mountain dogs, or Berners, are often noticed for their striking, tricolor coats. The medium-length hair can be straight or slightly wavy. It is jet-black and accented with white and rust-colored markings.

- **Height:** 23 to 27 inches (58 to 69 cm)
- **Weight:** 70 to 115 pounds (32 to 52 kg)

DID YOU KNOW?

When it is alert, the Berner carries its bushy tail with an upward curl. It carries its tail low when it is resting.

BEHAVIOR

Berners are good-natured animals. These gentle giants are self-confident, calm, affectionate, and smart. Although Berners are natural watchdogs, they are not aggressive unless threatened.

SPECIAL CONSIDERATIONS

The Berner is naturally suited for cold weather. In hot weather, its thick coat and large size can cause overheating. This can make a Berner very ill.

BREED HISTORY

No one knows exactly when the Bernese mountain dog breed began. Bernese mountain dogs are named for the Swiss state of Bern. The Bernese Alps are in this area.

BOXER AKC DATE: 1904

APPEARANCE

The boxer has a short, hard coat. They can be fawn, brindle, or white. Many boxers have white markings on their necks, chests, bellies, and feet.

- **Height:** 21 to 25 inches (53 to 64 cm)
- **Weight:** 50 to 80 pounds (23 to 36 kg)

DID YOU KNOW?

Boxers were one of the first dog breeds used in German police work. Today, boxers help with search and rescue work. And some boxers serve as service dogs to people with disabilities.

BEHAVIOR

Boxers are smart and playful dogs with lots of energy. They are alert and loyal. They can be good watchdogs. In the face of danger, boxers are very brave. But some boxers may fight with dogs that they do not know.

BREED HISTORY

Boxers have been around since the late 1800s. They were bred from a mix of bulldogs and mastiffs. Early on, butchers used boxers to help control cattle. People also used boxers in dogfights before the fights were outlawed.

DOBERMAN PINSCHER AKC DATE: 1908

APPEARANCE

The Doberman pinscher's coat is short and coarse. It can be black, red, blue, or fawn. All Dobermans have well-defined, rust-colored markings.

- **Height:** 24 to 28 inches (61 to 71 cm)
- **Weight:** 60 to 100 pounds (27 to 45 kg)

BEHAVIOR

The breed's guardian instincts have made Dobermans popular for military and police work. Doberman pinschers can also be loving family members. This social breed prefers to be indoors. It is curious and wants to be included in family activities.

DID YOU KNOW?

Some people crop Doberman pinschers' ears. The ears stand erect and pointed. They also dock the Doberman pinschers' tail so it is short. When not cropped, the Doberman pinschers' natural ears fold over in a manner similar to a hound's ears, and their natural tails are similar in length to other dogs of similar size.

BREED HISTORY

The Doberman pinscher originated in Germany in the late 1800s.

SPECIAL CONSIDERATIONS

Dobermans need outdoor areas to roam and run freely.

GREAT DANE AKC DATE: 1887

APPEARANCE

The Great Dane's coat is short and dense. Its hair is smooth and glossy. The AKC recognizes various Great Dane colors and patterns, including black, brindle, fawn, merle, white, silver, blue and white, and black and white.

- **Height:** 28 to 32 inches (71 to 81 cm)
- **Weight:** 110 to 175 pounds (50 to 80 kg)

DID YOU KNOW?

Cropping is cutting a Great Dane's ears so they come to a point. The dog's ears are then taped to stand up straight. After a while, the ears stand up without help. Usually after a Great Dane puppy is seven weeks old, a veterinarian will crop its ears.

BEHAVIOR

Great Danes can be wary of strangers. These dogs are not usually aggressive, but they do need strict training as puppies. With proper training and treatment, Great Danes are gentle and well-behaved. This breed can be very sensitive. They enjoy being inside a home and part of a family.

BREED HISTORY

People have bred Great Danes for nearly 400 years. Many people believe that this breed began in Denmark. That's because people from Denmark are called Danes. But in fact, this breed actually began in Germany.

SPECIAL CONSIDERATIONS

A Great Dane's ears need regular cleaning. Clean ears are less likely to become infected.

GREATER SWISS MOUNTAIN DOG
AKC DATE: 1995

APPEARANCE

The Greater Swiss mountain dog, or Swissy, has a dense double coat. Some have a black, white, and red coat. They can also be blue, white, and tan. Others are red and white.

- **Height:** 24 to 29 inches (61 to 74 cm)
- **Weight:** 85 to 140 pounds (39 to 64 kg)

BEHAVIOR

The Greater Swiss mountain dog is calm, friendly, and social. It likes to stick close to its family. This canine is a natural guard dog. It is wary of strangers and always on the alert.

DID YOU KNOW?

The Greater Swiss mountain dog is sometimes called a "gentle giant."

BREED HISTORY

About 2,000 years ago, Julius Caesar's army crossed the Alps to invade Gaul. The soldiers in his army brought trained mastiffs with them. Over time, these war dogs were bred into four new mountain dog breeds. The Swissy is the oldest and largest of them.

SPECIAL CONSIDERATIONS

This breed is at risk for certain medical issues. Bloat and incontinence are common.

MASTIFF AKC DATE: 1885

APPEARANCE

The mastiff comes in apricot, brindle, and fawn. The apricot and fawn coats are shades of light brown and white. The brindle pattern has an apricot or fawn background color covered with dark streaks.

- **Height:** 27 to 30 inches (69 to 76 cm) and up
- **Weight:** 120 to 230 pounds (54 to 104 kg)

DID YOU KNOW?

In 1989, a mastiff named Zorba appeared in the Guinness Book of World Records as the world's largest dog. He weighed an amazing 343 pounds (156 kg).

BEHAVIOR

Mastiffs need to be socialized to keep from becoming too shy. Mastiffs make marvelous watchdogs. They will naturally protect their homes. Mastiffs are gentle with those they love.

BREED HISTORY

Mastiffs may have originated in parts of Asia, such as Tibet and northern India. Large dogs similar to mastiffs are mentioned in the documents and legends of cultures across the world.

SPECIAL CONSIDERATIONS

This breed should avoid brisk exercise until they are at least 18 months old. Their bodies are still growing. Too much exercise will stress their bones and muscles.

NEWFOUNDLAND AKC DATE: 1886

APPEARANCE

The Newfoundland's coat is thick and moderately long. Standard colors are black, brown, gray, and Landseer. The Landseer Newfoundland has a white base coat with black markings.

- **Height:** 26 to 28 inches (66 to 71 cm)
- **Weight:** 100 to 150 pounds (45 to 68 kg)

DID YOU KNOW?

Because of their size, Newfoundlands should be trained and socialized at an early age. Obedience training teaches Newfoundlands to adjust their strength. This helps them avoid injuring anyone.

BEHAVIOR

Newfoundlands are patient and calm. They have a sweet temperament. They are also smart. This makes them easy to train.

152

BREED HISTORY

Where Newfoundlands came from is a mystery. However, historians agree the breed began in Newfoundland, Canada. Many believe fishermen brought the dog's ancestors to the area in the 1600s.

SPECIAL CONSIDERATIONS

Regular exercise is important for the health and well-being of Newfoundlands. Also, their thick coats and large size make it important to watch for heatstroke.

PORTUGUESE WATER DOG AKC DATE: 1983

APPEARANCE

Portuguese water dogs have naturally waterproof coats. Their coats can be either curly or wavy. Coat colors can be solid black, brown, or white. Or, they can combine black or brown with white.

- **Height:** 17 to 23 inches (43 to 58 cm)
- **Weight:** 35 to 60 pounds (16 to 27 kg)

DID YOU KNOW?

Portuguese water dogs were bred to work on fishing boats. These excellent swimmers helped herd fish into fishermen's nets.

BEHAVIOR

Portuguese water dogs are intelligent, loyal, obedient, and hardworking. They are strong enough to swim all day, and they are excellent divers.

BREED HISTORY

It is believed that the Portuguese water dog's ancestors came from the border area between Russia and China. These ancient dogs herded cattle, sheep, camels, and horses.

SPECIAL CONSIDERATIONS

Portuguese water dogs require lots of activity and attention. They need both physical and mental exercise.

ROTTWEILER AKC DATE: 1931

APPEARANCE

Rottweilers have a black outercoat. It has mahogany, rust, or tan markings.

- **Height:** 22 to 27 inches (56 to 69 cm)
- **Weight:** 80 to 135 pounds (36 to 61 kg)

DID YOU KNOW?

These intelligent dogs excel at police work, service work, and ranch work.

BEHAVIOR

Rottweilers love to show off and please their owners. Rottweilers are friendly toward their families and friends. But they are protective of their people and their territories. They do not welcome strangers.

BREED HISTORY

Historians believe that the Rottweiler is the descendant of herding dogs. In AD 74, these dogs accompanied Roman soldiers into what would become Rottweil in southern Germany. Their jobs were to herd and guard the livestock that the soldiers kept for food.

SPECIAL CONSIDERATIONS

Rottweilers can be aggressive. Obedience training and socialization are a must for these devoted animals.

SAINT BERNARD AKC DATE: 1885

APPEARANCE

Saint Bernards can have short or long coats. Short coats are smooth and thick. Long coats may have some wavy hair. Saint Bernards have patches of brown on their coats.

- **Height:** 26 to 30 inches (66 to 76 cm)
- **Weight:** 120 to 180 pounds (54 to 82 kg)

DID YOU KNOW?

Because of their droopy mouths, Saint Bernards drool. They drool when they exercise, when they're hot, and when they eat. They even drool when they are excited.

BEHAVIOR

Saint Bernards are gentle, easygoing dogs. They are patient, smart, and loyal. Saint Bernards love to be around people. With the right training, Saint Bernards are obedient. But some can be stubborn.

SPECIAL CONSIDERATIONS

Saint Bernards cannot handle hot weather. They can get heatstroke.

BREED HISTORY

Long ago, the only way to cross the Swiss Alps was through a snowy mountain pass that got a lot of snow. Many people got lost in the snow and died. Monks who lived in the area used huge dogs to help them find and rescue people. These dogs were later called Saint Bernards.

SAMOYED AKC DATE: 1906

APPEARANCE

The Samoyed has a dense double coat designed for Arctic winters. The coat can be white, biscuit, white and biscuit, or cream.

- **Height:** 19 to 23.5 inches (48 to 60 cm)
- **Weight:** 35 to 65 pounds (16 to 29 kg)

DID YOU KNOW?

Its heavy-duty coat lets the Samoyed endure temperatures as low as -60 degrees Fahrenheit (-51°C).

BEHAVIOR

This breed is known for its friendly, loyal personality. It's a real people pleaser and forms a tight bond with its family. These dogs are also very talkative. They often bark, howl, and sing.

BREED HISTORY

Samoyeds originated hundreds of years ago in northwestern Siberia. They were used to pull heavy sleds and herd reindeer.

SPECIAL CONSIDERATIONS

The Samoyed sheds heavily year-round. And twice a year it sheds even more to remove its thick undercoat.

SIBERIAN HUSKY AKC DATE: 1930

APPEARANCE

Siberian huskies have a double coat. The outercoat is straight, silky, and smooth. Under that is a very soft, thick undercoat. The color can be anything from very white to mostly black. Their eyes can be brown, blue, or one of each.

- **Height:** 20 to 23 inches (51 to 58 cm)
- **Weight:** 35 to 60 pounds (16 to 27 kg)

DID YOU KNOW?

Siberian huskies are able to work in temperatures as low as -75 degrees Fahrenheit (-59°C).

BEHAVIOR

Siberian huskies are gentle and playful. They are very good with children and friendly with strangers. In fact, they are so friendly that they don't make very good guard dogs.

BREED HISTORY

Siberian huskies started in Siberia, one of the coldest places in the world. They were brought to Alaska in 1909 by fur traders and were often used in sled dog races.

SPECIAL CONSIDERATIONS

Siberian huskies need a lot of exercise. However, they should not be outside in very hot weather for long periods of time.

ADDITIONAL BREEDS IN THE GROUP

AKITA

- **What It's Known For:** Hunting and guarding
- **Where It Comes From:** Japan
- **Special Considerations:** This breed is sometimes intolerant when it comes to other animals.

ANATOLIAN SHEPHERD DOG

- **What It's Known For:** Guarding
- **Where It Comes From:** Anatolia
- **Special Considerations:** This breed is protective and should be socialized.

BOERBOEL

- **What It's Known For:** Guarding
- **Where It Comes From:** South Africa
- **Special Considerations:** This breed might not get along well with other dogs and is very protective.

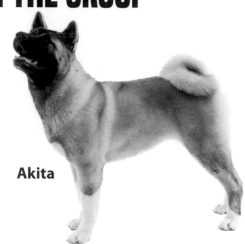

Akita

BULLMASTIFF

- **What It's Known For:** Protecting and companionship
- **Where It Comes From:** England
- **Special Considerations:** This breed is energetic and needs exercise every day.

CANE CORSO

- **What It's Known For:** Guarding
- **Where It Comes From:** Italy
- **Special Considerations:** This breed needs a lot of exercise.

CHINOOK

- **What It's Known For:** Hauling heavy loads
- **Where It Comes From:** United States
- **Special Considerations:** This breed is energetic and needs exercise.

Boerboel

DOGUE DE BORDEAUX

- **What It's Known For:** Guarding
- **Where It Comes From:** France
- **Special Considerations:** Owners of these dogs should check the dogs' wrinkles often to make sure they are dry and clean.

GERMAN PINSCHER

- **What It's Known For:** Hunting and guarding
- **Where It Comes From:** Germany
- **Special Considerations:** This breed is intelligent and has high energy.

German pinscher

Cane Corso

GREAT PYRENEES

- **What It's Known For:** Guarding
- **Where It Comes From:** The border of Spain and France
- **Special Considerations:** This breed is independent.

KOMONDOR

- **What It's Known For:** Guarding
- **Where It Comes From:** Hungary
- **Special Considerations:** This breed needs specialty grooming.

KUVASZ

- **What It's Known For:** Guarding
- **Where It Comes From:** Hungary
- **Special Considerations:** This breed is independent.

OTHER DOGS

There are hundreds of different dogs, and not all are recognized by the AKC or are placed into a specific group. Some dogs are mixed breeds. Because they are not purebred, these dogs cannot be recognized by the AKC.

There are many different mixed breeds. For instance, the goldendoodle is a mix of a golden retriever and poodle. And puggles are a mix of a pug and beagle. Mixed breeds are less predictable in appearance and behavior compared with purebred dogs.

Puggle

Goldendoodle

COCKAPOO

APPEARANCE

Cockapoos blend the qualities of the poodle with those of the cocker spaniel. Cockapoo hair can be curly, wavy, or flat. They can be many colors including black, white, apricot, chocolate, cream, red, and silver. Cockapoos are often broken into three or four size groups. Standard is the largest and teacup is the smallest.

- **Height:** A cockapoo's size is based on the size of its poodle parent.
- **Weight:** Cockapoos can weigh anywhere from less than 12 pounds (5 kg) to more than 20 pounds (9 kg).

BEHAVIOR

Cockapoos are friendly, loving, and eager to please. Cockapoos are generally well-behaved around children. They also are good around other pets, especially if they first meet when the cockapoos are puppies.

HISTORY

Cockapoos have been bred since the 1950s. People loved the sweet, patient dogs that resulted from breeding a poodle with a cocker spaniel.

There are two different kinds of cockapoos. The American cockapoo is a cross between a poodle and an American cocker spaniel. The English cockapoo is a cross between a poodle and an English cocker spaniel.

GOLDENDOODLE

APPEARANCE

Goldendoodles are a mix of golden retrievers and poodles. Goldendoodle coats can range from the soft, wavy fluff of a golden retriever coat to the tight curls of a poodle coat. Goldendoodles have been bred in cream, apricot, red, black, blue, and even chocolate.

- **Height:** 13 to 24 inches (33 to 61 cm) or more
- **Weight:** 15 to 100 pounds (7 to 45 kg)

BEHAVIOR

Goldendoodles are smart dogs. They are not territorial. Like their parent breeds, goldendoodles enjoy retrieving games. They also love water. Goldendoodles are easy to train.

DID YOU KNOW?

Some goldendoodles are guide dogs. Others have also been trained as sniffer dogs.

HISTORY

People began breeding goldendoodles in the 1990s. Usually, the name is credited to golden retriever breeder Amy Lane of West Virginia. Lane bred a male poodle to one of her golden retrievers.

SPECIAL CONSIDERATIONS

Goldendoodle owners must provide their dogs with plenty of attention. They need a lot of time with people.

LABRADOODLE

APPEARANCE

Labradoodles are a mix of lab and poodle. Many have either fleece or wool coats. They can come in many colors. These include black, gold, apricot, red, cream, chocolate, and silver.

- **Height:** 14 to 24 inches (36 to 61 cm)
- **Weight:** 15 to 65 pounds (7 to 30 kg)

DID YOU KNOW?

Labradoodles that spend a lot of time outside may have lighter-colored coats on top. This is from the sun.

BEHAVIOR

Labradoodles are sociable and friendly. They are extremely loyal to their families. Labradoodles are smart and easy to train. Obedience training is a good idea, as is some activity each day. Like any smart dog, Labradoodles can get into trouble if they become bored.

HISTORY

An Australian man named Wally Conron bred the first Labradoodles in 1989.

SPECIAL CONSIDERATIONS

Labradoodle owners need to take care of the dog's coat. Otherwise, it could get matted around the dog's whole body.

MUTT

APPEARANCE

A mutt is a dog that does not have two purebred parents of the same breed. Mutts have a variety of coat types. They can have wavy or straight coats. The hair can be long or short. It may even change as the dogs age. Coat color also varies in mutts. These special dogs come in dozens of colors and patterns.

Like its coat type, a mutt's size is also hard to determine when the parent breeds are unknown. Mutt sizes range from very small to extra large.

DID YOU KNOW?

Many people believe mutts are stronger, better tempered, and healthier than purebreds. Some people also think mutts are smarter. However, these claims have not been proven.

BEHAVIOR

The surprise of a mutt's build or look is what many owners love. Personality, size, color, and shape vary from dog to dog.

SPECIAL CONSIDERATIONS

People might not know what they will get with a mutt in terms of temperament and appearance.

HISTORY

As dogs began splitting off from wolves, there were no dog breeds. Over time, people began breeding dogs to strengthen certain skills, such as hunting and guarding. Through careful breeding, early dogs developed into the purebred dogs we know today. A purebred dog's gene pool is well documented. Its ancestors are the same breed. And its heritage can be traced back for generations. A mutt has an unknown mix of genes. Its ancestors can come from many breeds.

PUGGLE

APPEARANCE

Puggles are a mix between beagles and pugs. Puggles can be fawn, tan, red, black, or white. Some are a solid color. Others are a mixture of colors.

- **Height:** 8 to 15 inches (20 to 38 cm)
- **Weight:** 15 to 30 pounds (7 to 14 kg)

DID YOU KNOW?

Like beagles, puggles often bark at strangers or unfamiliar animals. They may also howl if they are left alone for too long. However, most puggles bark and howl less than purebred beagles.

BEHAVIOR

The puggle has a lot of energy. Its beagle background may make it eager for a walk each day to burn off energy. However, its pug background means it is equally happy to plop down for a nap. Like both the beagle and the pug, the puggle is very social. And just like its pug parent, the puggle wants lots of attention.

HISTORY

No one is certain where the first puggles were bred. Some people believe the first planned puggles were bred in the 1980s in Wisconsin.

SPECIAL CONSIDERATIONS

It is important to clean a puggle's ears to prevent infection.

SCHNOODLE

APPEARANCE

Schnoodles are a mix of schnauzers and poodles. Most schnoodles are gray, silver, or black. They can also be brown, white, or apricot. A schnoodle's mother can be one of three different sizes. So can its father. That leads to a lot of variety in schnoodle sizes.

Toy schnoodles
- **Height:** 10 to 12 inches (25 to 30 cm)
- **Weight:** 6 to 10 pounds (3 to 4.5 kg)

Miniature schnoodles
- **Height:** 12 to 15 inches (30 to 38 cm)
- **Weight:** 13 to 20 pounds (6 to 9 kg)

Standard schnoodles
- **Height:** 15 to 26 inches (38 to 66 cm)
- **Weight:** 20 to 75 pounds (9 to 34 kg)

BEHAVIOR

Schnoodle owners say their dogs are loving, loyal, happy, and protective. However, the personality of a particular schnoodle depends on its background. Schnoodles can be quite active.

DID YOU KNOW?

Some schnoodles have the ear position of a schnauzer, but the finer bones of a poodle.

SPECIAL CONSIDERATIONS

Schnoodles with soft, wavy coats need weekly brushing. Schnoodles with poodle-like coats require a haircut at least every couple of months.

HISTORY

No one knows who bred the original schnoodle. It is believed that the schnoodle made its first appearance during the 1980s.

YORKIE-POO

APPEARANCE

A Yorkie-poo blends the qualities of a toy or miniature poodle with those of the Yorkshire terrier. Yorkie-poos have soft, silky, low-shedding coats. Yorkie-poos also come in a variety of colors.

- **Height:** 7 to 15 inches (18 to 38 cm)
- **Weight:** 3 to 14 pounds (1 to 6 kg)

BEHAVIOR

Yorkie-poos are smart, friendly, and curious. They have high energy levels. Yorkie-poos are happy dogs that love to have fun. They do not like to be left out of family activities.

DID YOU KNOW?

Both poodles and Yorkies make good watchdogs. So do Yorkie-poos. Like Yorkies and poodles, Yorkie-poos like to bark.

HISTORY

Poodle mixes have become very popular since the 1990s. Smaller dogs have also become more in demand. Breeders crossed miniature and toy poodles with Yorkshire terriers and created the Yorkie-poo.

SPECIAL CONSIDERATIONS

The Yorkie-poo's soft, silky coat needs daily brushing and combing. Otherwise, it may become matted. It also is important to keep the Yorkie-poo's hair from growing into its eyes.

ADDITIONAL BREEDS

The AKC has a miscellaneous group filled with more purebred dogs. However, these dogs are still waiting to be fully recognized by the AKC.

Bracco Italiano

BRACCO ITALIANO

- **What It's Known For:** Hunting
- **Where It Comes From:** Unknown
- **Special Considerations:** These dogs like to be around people.

DUTCH SHEPHERD

- **What It's Known For:** Herding
- **Where It Comes From:** Netherlands
- **Special Considerations:** These dogs are smart and need exercise.

LANCASHIRE HEELER

- **What It's Known For:** Hunting rats and herding
- **Where It Comes From:** Unknown
- **Special Considerations:** These dogs need physical exercise and mental stimulation.

MUDI

- **What It's Known For:** Herding
- **Where It Comes From:** Hungary
- **Special Considerations:** These dogs have a lot of energy.

NORRBOTTENSPETS

- **What It's Known For:** Hunting
- **Where It Comes From:** Finland and Sweden
- **Special Considerations:** These dogs are energetic.

Lancashire heeler

PERUVIAN INCA ORCHID

- **What It's Known For:** Sighthound
- **Where It Comes From:** Peru
- **Special Considerations:** If outside in the sun, the hairless variety needs sunscreen.

PORTUGUESE PODENGO

- **What It's Known For:** Hunting
- **Where It Comes From:** Portugal
- **Special Considerations:** These dogs are watchful and might not be as playful with strangers.

Mudi

RUSSIAN TOY

- **What It's Known For:** Companionship
- **Where It Comes From:** Russia
- **Special Considerations:** These dogs like lots of attention from people.

TEDDY ROOSEVELT TERRIER

- **What It's Known For:** Hunting vermin
- **Where It Comes From:** United States
- **Special Considerations:** This dog is protective.

Russian toy

DOG CARE

GROOMING

There are many different types of dogs. Because of this, dogs have different grooming needs. Some need to be brushed frequently to avoid matting. Others have so little hair that they need sunscreen when in the sun. It's important to research what each dog specifically needs in order to have them look their best and stay healthy.

FOOD AND WATER

Whatever its breed, each dog has its own dietary needs. They depend on the dog's age, size, and activity level. Overfeeding is harmful.

Dog food can be dry, moist, or semimoist. Most dogs will eat a high-quality dry dog food. Others prefer to have some canned food mixed in with their dry food. Work with your vet to choose a nutritious food that your dog enjoys and stick with it. Changes in diet should be made gradually to prevent stomach problems.

Dog owners should always have a bowl of clean, fresh water available for their pets to drink. Just like you, dogs especially need a drink during hot weather or after exercising.

Many dogs should be brushed often to keep their coats healthy.

REGULAR VET CHECKUPS

Dogs should visit the veterinarian at least once a year for a checkup. The veterinarian can check dogs for illnesses and give them shots to prevent diseases.

SAFETY AND IDENTIFICATION

All dogs need a collar with an identification tag. If your dog gets lost, an ID tag will provide a way for you to be contacted. A vet can also insert a microchip in your new pet. The chip will help identify your pet.

OTHER SUPPLIES

Other supplies for dogs can include a crate, bed, and lots of toys.

Pet owners should take care of their dog's teeth.

GLOSSARY

bloat
A condition in which food and gas trapped in a dog's stomach cause pain, shock, and even death.

breed
A group of animals sharing the same ancestors and appearance. To breed animals is to mate the animals together in order to get offspring. People who do this are called breeders.

brindle
A gray, tan, or tawny color with darker streaks or spots.

crop
To cut the ears of a dog so they stand up instead of flop.

dense
Thick or compact.

dock
To cut the tail of a dog to a shorter length.

Gaul
An ancient European country that is now France and parts of Belgium, Germany, and Italy.

incontinence
The inability to control the release of urine from the body.

liver
A reddish-brown color.

mat
A tangled mass.

merle
A pattern of dark patches of color on a lighter background.

microchip
An electronic circuit placed under an animal's skin. A microchip contains identifying information that can be read by a scanner.

sable
A pattern of black-tipped hairs with a silver, gold, gray, fawn, or brown base.

FURTHER READINGS

Baines, Becky. *Everything Dogs*. National Geographic Society, 2012.

The Dog Encyclopedia: The Definitive Visual Guide. DK Publishing, 2013.

Hajeski, Nancy J. *Every Dog: The Ultimate Guide to Over 450 Dog Breeds*. Firefly Books, 2016.

ONLINE RESOURCES

To learn more about dogs, please visit **abdobooklinks.com** or scan this QR code. These links are routinely monitored and updated to provide the most current information available.

INDEX

PHOTO CREDITS

Previously titled The Dog Encyclopedia for Kids

First Edition
First Paperback Printing, 2022

THIS BOOK CONTAINS
RECYCLED MATERIALS

Editor: Alyssa Sorenson
Series Designer: Colleen McLaren
Cover Designer: Karli Kruse

ISBN: 978-1-952455-01-8 (paperback)

Library of Congress Control Number: 2022901692

Distributed in paperback by North Star Editions, Inc.
2297 Waters Drive
Mendota Heights, MN 55120
www.northstareditions.com

Printed in the United States of America